35444000560820
971.0622092 KIN
Levine, Allan
King : William Lyon
Mackenzie King : a life

D0759529

King

Also by
Allan Levine

NON-FICTION

THE EXCHANGE:
100 Years of Trading Grain in Winnipeg

YOUR WORSHIP:
The Lives of Eight of Canada's Most Unforgettable Mayors (editor)

SCRUM WARS:
The Prime Ministers and the Media

FUGITIVES OF THE FOREST:
The Heroic Story of Jewish Resistance and Survival During the Second World War

SCATTERED AMONG THE PEOPLES:
The Jewish Diaspora in Ten Portraits

THE DEVIL IN BABYLON:
Fear of Progress and the Birth of Modern Life

COMING OF AGE:
A History of the Jewish People of Manitoba

FICTION: HISTORICAL MYSTERIES

THE BLOOD LIBEL

SINS OF THE SUFFRAGETTE

THE BOLSHEVIK'S REVENGE

EVIL OF THE AGE